MILITARY MANPOWER and NATIONAL SECURITY

*A Statement on National Policy
by the Research and Policy Committee
of the Committee for Economic Development
February, 1972*

CED

Single copy ... $1.00

Printed in U.S.A.
First Printing February 1972
Design: Harry Carter
Library of Congress Catalog Card Number: 78-189538
International Standard Book Number: 0-87186-045-7

Committee for Economic Development
477 Madison Avenue, New York, N.Y. 10022

★ Contents ★

The Responsibility for
CED Statements on National Policy

This statement has been approved for publication as a statement of the Research and Policy Committee by the members of that Committee and its drafting sub-committee, subject to individual dissents or reservations noted herein. The trustees who are responsible for this statement are listed on the opposite page. Company associations are included for identification only; the companies do not share in the responsibility borne by the individuals.

The Research and Policy Committee is directed by CED's bylaws to:

"Initiate studies into the principles of business policy and of public policy which will foster the full contribution by industry and commerce to the attainment and maintenance of high and secure standards of living for people in all walks of life through maximum employment and high productivity in the domestic economy."

The bylaws emphasize that:

"All research is to be thoroughly objective in character, and the approach in each instance is to be from the standpoint of the general welfare and not from that of any special political or economic group."

The Research and Policy Committee is composed of 60 Trustees from among the 200 businessmen and educators who comprise the Committee for Economic Development. It is aided by a Research Advisory Board of leading economists, a small permanent Research Staff, and by advisors chosen for their competence in the field being considered.

Each Statement on National Policy is preceded by discussions, meetings, and exchanges of memoranda, often stretching over many months. The research is undertaken by a subcommittee, with its advisors, and the full Research and Policy Committee participates in the drafting of findings and recommendations.

Except for the members of the Research and Policy Committee and the responsible subcommittee, the recommendations presented herein are not necessarily endorsed by other Trustees or by the advisors, contributors, staff members, or others associated with CED.

The Research and Policy Committee offers these Statements on National Policy as an aid to clearer understanding of the steps to be taken in achieving sustained growth of the American economy. The Committee is not attempting to pass on any pending specific legislative proposals; its purpose is to urge careful consideration of the objectives set forth in the statement and of the best means of accomplishing those objectives.

4.

5.

PROJECT DIRECTOR

THOMAS C. SCHELLING
Center for International Affairs
Harvard University

ADVISORS TO THE SUBCOMMITTEE

MORTON HALPERIN
The Brookings Institution

CHARLES P. KINDLEBERGER
Department of Economics and Social Science
Massachusetts Institute of Technology

EDWARD S. MASON
Lamont University Professor
Harvard University

FREDERICK C. MOSHER
Woodrow Wilson Department of Government
and Foreign Affairs
University of Virginia

CHARLES L. SCHULTZE
The Brookings Institution

DONALD C. STONE
Graduate School of Public and
International Affairs
University of Pittsburgh

CED Staff Advisors

SOL HURWITZ
ROBERT F. LENHART
FRANK W. SCHIFF

RESEARCH ADVISORY BOARD

Chairman
CHARLES L. SCHULTZE
The Brookings Institution

EDWARD C. BANFIELD
Department of Government
Harvard University

ALAN K. CAMPBELL
Dean, The Maxwell School of Citizenship
and Public Affairs
Syracuse University

WILBUR J. COHEN
Dean, School of Education
The University of Michigan

WALTER W. HELLER
Department of Economics
University of Minnesota

LAWRENCE C. HOWARD
Dean, Graduate School of Public
and International Affairs
University of Pittsburgh

CARL KAYSEN
Director, The Institute for
Advanced Study
Princeton University

JOHN R. MEYER
President
National Bureau of Economic Research, Inc.

FREDERICK C. MOSHER
Woodrow Wilson Department of
Government and Foreign Affairs
University of Virginia

DON K. PRICE
Dean, John Fitzgerald Kennedy School
of Government
Harvard University

RAYMOND VERNON
Graduate School
of Business Administration
Harvard University

HENRY C. WALLICH
Department of Economics
Yale University

Associate Members
CHARLES P. KINDLEBERGER
Department of Economics
and Social Science
Massachusetts Institute of Technology

MITCHELL SVIRIDOFF
Vice President, Division
of National Affairs
The Ford Foundation

PAUL N. YLVISAKER
Professor, Public Affairs and
Urban Planning
Woodrow Wilson School of Public
and International Affairs
Princeton University

6.

★ Foreword ★

The concern of the CED Research and Policy Committee with national security decisions arises from the major impact which military spending has had upon the growth and stability of the United States economy and upon the allocation of resources for urgent domestic needs. The importance of the military sector of the economy is illustrated by a defense budget of over 75 billion dollars a year and the employment of some four million men and women.

The Subcommittee on Decision Making for National Security, which prepared this statement, devoted about a year to a review of the military decision-making process. Out of this review came the Subcommittee's conclusion that one of the most important ways to improve national security decisions is through analysis, debate, and legislative action on the procurement and deployment of military manpower.

The statement in the following pages, therefore, is not a comprehensive treatment of defense management. Rather, it attempts to appraise systematically several critical issues which demand attention. The statement draws together two separate but closely related problems involving the men and women who are at the center of our military establishment and who account for more than half of the military budget. The first question deals with manpower policies, including the draft and long-term procedures for the recruitment and management of military personnel. The second is the question of accountability, focusing on

7.

ways in which Congress might assume greater responsibility for the commitment of military manpower.

Underlying the recommendations of this policy statement is our awareness that basic decisions about military commitments are seldom exposed sufficiently to public discussion and debate. It is our belief that important improvements will occur only when a framework is established which generates an informed dialogue. The statement's proposal for an annual military manpower review attempts to provide such a framework.

At the same time, serious consideration was given to the opposing views of those who felt that an increased Congressional role would seriously weaken the flexibility of the Executive Branch in guiding the nation through an unstable and volatile world situation. The Committee took steps to insure that its recommendations would preserve the ability of the President to deal with emergencies rapidly and firmly in times of peace as well as in times of war.

We recognize that there will be occasions when a stronger Congressional role will conflict with the powers of a President. However, we believe that on balance this risk is warranted. Events of recent years have shown that the ability of the President to conduct foreign policy depends not only on his formal powers but on the support he has at home. It is only with the support of Congress and the American people that the President can shape a truly effective foreign policy.

In the coming months the Subcommittee intends to continue its work in the area of defense decision making and to give further attention to the national defense budget.

I should like to extend the appreciation of the Research and Policy Committee to all members of the Subcommittee which prepared the statement, particularly to Chairman William C. Foster and Vice Chairman Franklin A. Lindsay, as well as to the Subcommittee's advisors. Thomas C. Schelling, Project Director, deserves special recognition for the drafting of the statement.

We gratefully acknowledge the financial support for this study provided by the Carnegie Corporation of New York, the Rockefeller Brothers Fund, the W. K. Kellogg Foundation, and the Stern Fund.

Philip M. Klutznick, *Co-Chairman*
Research and Policy Committee

8.

1.

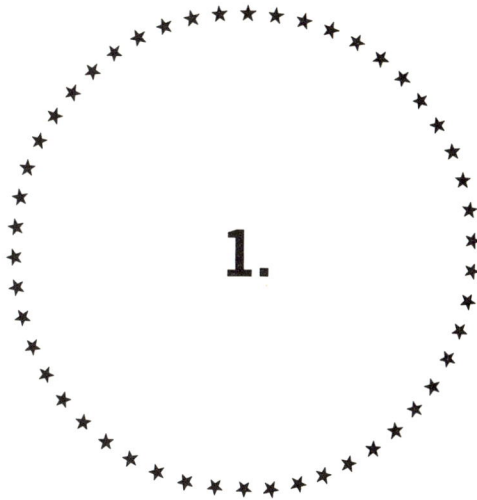

Manpower in the Framework of
National Security Decisions

The quest for improved organization, program procedures, and management in the field of national defense is never ending. Changing commitments and technologies, and the accumulation of experience—successful and unsuccessful—tend to make today's organization out-of-date tomorrow. Foreign policy and military affairs not only involve millions of men and billions of dollars, but are often full of uncertainties, burdened with secrecy, and exposed to emotions and special interests. As a result, there is no ideal logic by which to relate programs and resources to well-defined and appropriately weighted strategic objectives.*

We are aware that there are limits to the success with which any large, complex enterprise can be managed toward a set of competing and sometimes conflicting goals, especially when an electorate is divided as to the resources it will commit and the goals it will pursue. But we doubt that those limits have been reached. We doubt also that any ideal structure for national security decisions can be devised. It is for prag-

---

*See Memoranda by MR. JOSEPH COORS on page 38, and by MR. RICHARD C. GERSTENBERG on page 39.

matic reasons, therefore, that we have focused in this statement on "military manpower." It is a large unit that can be effectively dealt with in an integrated fashion, and it is one that lends itself to the stimulation of debate on the broader issues of public policy. For purposes of analysis, military manpower issues cluster in a way that economizes time and information. They bring together problems that must be resolved jointly because of their interdependence. They involve a major resource —people—that has unique characteristics. And they account for a major category of the defense budget.

Analyzing Manpower Programs

An important effort has been made in the last ten years, first in the Department of Defense and then in many civilian agencies, to budget by "program" rather than by a series of "inputs." The military services, it can be said, have no need for a particular total of manpower; they need various mixtures of resources, including manpower, in the several major programs related to the several tasks and responsibilities that they must undertake. The Strategic Air Command needs men; the Sixth Fleet needs men; the U.S. forces committed to NATO need men; and the manpower total should logically flow from the consideration of these major programs. And that total should not be accorded special significance by itself, any more than the totals for fuel or ammunition should have separate significance. *Input* totals, it can be argued, should always be derived from program objectives; they are the *result* of an analysis that focuses on objectives; they are derived from those objectives and should not themselves be the focus of analysis. They are the means, not the purpose.

But there are different perspectives and different ways to look at the whole. While the Marines guarding an embassy in Latin America have little strategic relation to the men who tend ships' boilers in the Sixth Fleet or man radar stations in Alaska, for purposes of management they are part of an interconnected system. In terms of pay, privileges, retirement, social status, legal rights, and a variety of other things that matter to them, they are bound together as a "personnel system" even though they are sharply separated by the strategic objectives they serve.

10.

The Uniqueness of Troop Authorizations

Furthermore there are two characteristics of men and women in uniform that make dollar values a poor measure of costs, so that in the budgetary process they cannot be merely represented as "personnel expenditures." One is that men are drafted—required to serve regardless of their preferences and at a rate of pay that clearly did not attract them into military service. The ships, fuel, and ammunition, the construction and the transport, are largely procured in the marketplace. Draftees are not. The draft is a levy in kind on the young men who serve. The word "conscription" describes it: it is a tax that fails to show in the receipts when collected, and correspondingly fails to show in the expenses as budgeted. The men involved are human resources and the fact that they may be serving involuntarily entails responsibilities that do not arise in ordinary procurement.

The second distinguishing characteristic of men in uniform is the extreme significance attached to their presence in a country that did not provide the uniform. American troops in foreign countries, friendly or not, are more than mere "military assets." They are soldiers whose presence in those countries is construed differently from that of materiel by the governments concerned; and they entail responsibilities for the President as Commander-in-Chief that ordinary supplies and equipment do not entail. The significance of American troops overseas, particularly when equipped for combat, is often not only a matter of military strength. They symbolize the nation itself. Pragmatically, one of the best ways to examine American "commitments" is to examine the deployment of uniformed Americans around the globe and the respective responsibility of the President and the Congress for the commitment of military manpower.

Congressional Authority and Presidential Flexibility

There have been recent legislative attempts—none enacted yet—to spell out in detail the flexibility to be allowed the President in meeting military emergencies, and the power of Congress in providing advance authority to the President or in imposing specific limitations on him. It remains to be seen whether such specification is feasible. The possible contingencies are many and subtle; events do not fall into neat categories; inevitable loopholes may by implication increase flexibility where the intent was reduction. In any event the President typically has the initiative and the command, and the Congress is poor in techniques to discipline a President after the fact.

However, the Congress can do three things to reduce conflict and confusion and to exercise more fully and constructively its own Constitutional responsibilities. One is to be more concrete and explicit about the actions that have prior authorization—specifically the deployment of troops overseas. The second is to impose on the President a requirement for a prompt report to the Congress whenever he takes an action for which there is no prior authorization but for which, in his judgment, speed, secrecy, or other considerations made it infeasible to seek prior authorization. And the third is to be prompt itself, both in responding to the need for emergency legislation and in meeting its own schedule for annual legislative action.

We do not believe it wise, and doubt it possible, to keep an official authorized list of "commitments"—all of the obligations, explicit and implicit, that the United States has incurred abroad, or all the contingencies in which the government would feel obliged to act or want other countries to consider the United States obliged. Many commitments are hypothetical. Many are left ambiguous because of incomplete agreement. Any listing of "commitments" tends to denigrate those missing from the list, and may do more harm than good if it cannot be comprehensive.

An Annual Base Line

What we do think can be annually authorized is the hard physical fact of American citizens wearing the uniforms of the armed services, officially stationed on active duty abroad. While there are minor ambiguities about the "active-duty status" of soldiers in transit, on leave, on temporary duty, vacationing, or lent to civilian agencies, reasonable men can agree on whether or not American troops are deployed on foreign soil or in foreign territorial waters, and on an approximate average number. A significant change in their number or location is an observable fact.

Thus if the Congress wants to come to grips with the formation and activation of U.S. "commitments" abroad, the concrete facts of

12.

American military manpower provide a tangible opportunity. And if the numbers are authorized regularly and annually, there is always an up-to-date official answer to the question of what Congress has authorized. There is a base line for measuring departures. And there is a procedure for examining annually and reexamining these commitments without having to challenge every commitment or unduly to make an issue of it.

Resolving the Flexibility Issue

Congress clearly has the authority to provide or not to provide the military personnel. The possibility of a need for prompt action by the Commander-in-Chief is not in conflict with annually authorized troop levels and draft quotas, so long as the Congress can amend them on short notice during the year. On the deployment side of the ledger, the Congress can have an effective procedure for sharing responsibility with the President, without seeming to encroach on command decisions, but only if it has continually updated bench marks with respect to authorized military personnel overseas.

There may be specific limitations that the Congress would wish to impose, other than numbers of troops by geographical area. There may even be specific restrictions that the President would welcome being made firm and public. There will undoubtedly be a degree of conflict between the President and the Congress over the appropriate degree of flexibility.

But a prerequisite for Congressional effectiveness is a clear bench mark of what is already authorized in terms of concrete programs, specifically men in uniform deployed overseas. Clarity on this score can reduce tension between President and Congress, and misunderstanding abroad.

Strengthening both
the Executive and the Legislative Branches

There is always the danger that any procedure for establishing Congressional authority over matters as sensitive as troop deployment will be construed as an effort to redivide Legislative and Executive responsibility, apportioning more to the Congress and less to the President. But it would be a mistake to construe responsibility and authority as a fixed quantity to be divided between these two branches of the government.

A procedure by which the Congress can regularly authorize military manpower would not subtract from the credibility of the Executive Branch, or from its ability to act in emergencies. While it should strengthen the hand of the Congress, we expect and intend it simultaneously to strengthen the policy making of the U.S. government, and specifically the President's ability to conduct foreign policy.*

It must be acknowledged that, whether for sufficient or insufficient reasons, there has been a decline recently in the confidence of the American people and their Congressional leaders in the very procedures by which foreign policy is made. And this has led to a decline in confidence abroad that the President of the United States speaks for a unified nation. Doubts have been expressed, from both responsible and irresponsible sources, about the wisdom and efficacy of U.S. policy as well as the legitimacy of American military actions, deployments, and commitments overseas.

There has grown a widespread if not dominant feeling that the President and the Legislative Branch are at odds—not only with respect to the substance of military policy but with respect to authority and responsibility for incurring commitments and for meeting obligations. Even the term "Constitutional crisis" has lately come into use again to describe this situation.

A stronger Congressional participation in our military commitments and our military posture can reduce this division. There is no reason to believe that in the long run it is division rather than collaboration that will characterize Executive-Legislative relations in foreign policy.

The past few years have been marked by ad hoc Congressional efforts to gain or regain authority and influence over foreign policy. Most such efforts have involved at least an apparent challenge to the wisdom and even the legitimacy of Presidential actions. The last few years have been equally marked by efforts on the part of the President to assert the legitimacy of his actions, often at a time when a sharing of

*See Memorandum by MR. DONALD S. PERKINS, page 39.

14.

Executive and Legislative responsibility might have enhanced the stature of this country and its policies.

There would have to be compromise. But even a policy of compromise can be a stronger policy, from the viewpoint of both the President and the Congress, if there is a procedure for achieving compromise other than through a bitter adversary proceeding.

The Executive Branch has presently no clearly established procedure for having commitments scrutinized by the Congress and endorsed or acquiesced in. The Congress has no regular way of supporting commitments incurred by the President.

A regular procedure by which the Congress can go on record annually with the authorization of overseas troop commitments is a way of preventing every military policy consultation from becoming a confrontation. It is a way of making the Congress declare itself periodically when it might be easier to stand back and let the President take full responsibility. It is a way of permitting the President to acquire Congressional endorsement without making an extraordinary event out of his seeking such endorsement.

Undeniably there will be occasions when a stronger Congressional role in foreign policy will be in opposition to a President. But we do not believe that the Executive and Legislative Branches of our government are inherently partisan opponents and have nothing to gain from each other's strength. We particularly believe that only the two branches of government acting in concert—even if concert means compromise—can command the necessary sense of unity and legitimacy at home and the confident belief abroad that the United States is indeed a single and decisive entity in world affairs.

2.

The Draft in Perspective

The issue of the draft too often revolves around the question of whether the draft should be permanently continued or finally ended. But a larger question gets closer to the heart of the issue: how can the United States find a rational way to recruit and manage military manpower in the long run—a long run that will be composed of eventful short runs and that will always be full of uncertainties?

Draft reform is a matter of concern because the draft touches the lives of so many people and raises profound questions of fairness and obligation. There may well be aspects of the present draft law that are basically unsound, and potential changes that would represent unconditional improvements. But the process of draft *revision*, in contrast to "reform," is continuous. Any draft must be adapted to needs and circumstances.

Specifically, the terms and conditions of Selective Service should not be the same for an armed force of two and a quarter million as for an armed force of three and a half million. They should not be the same when men are being regularly sent into combat as when the country is at peace. They should not remain constant so long as the mix of skills and age groups is changing with the changing demands of technology and diplomacy, and with shifts between and within the different services. Revision of the Military Selective Service Act should not therefore be viewed as the occasional confrontation of two sides—those who like the draft as it was and those who have been continually discontented with it.

Length of Authorization

Nor should a one-year authorization imply an inability on the part of the Congress to make up its mind, or a promise or even suggestion that the draft will terminate after one year. During the 1971 Congressional hearings, concern was occasionally voiced that a one-year extension would mislead young men of draft age and others in the belief that the Congress foresaw an end to the draft or intended to end it after one year. There is no need for such an interpretation. The fault —and it is an easily correctable fault—is in the tradition of extending the draft four years at a time, with only occasional interim modifications, instead of regularly reviewing, just as with appropriated funds, the needs for the coming year.

No one supposes that defense expenditures are expected to come to a stop when the budget year is over. (Indeed, even the Constitution limits military appropriations to two years, and there has never been a presumption that no war could last longer.) A regular manpower review, with annual manpower and draft authorizations, could put an end to speculation about the likely duration of the draft based on the length of draft extension; it would preclude any need to choose a term of extension that represented anybody's estimate of how long the draft might last.

Putting each current-year proposal into the context of a three-year manpower projection would make explicit the Executive Branch's estimate of any draft requirements for the following year, and the Congressional committee appraisals of those foreseen requirements. Consequently, there would be a clearer basis than any that presently exists for an interested citizen to see what forecast regarding the draft underlies the year's legislative proposal.

17.

Ending the Draft

In the past few years the question has been seriously raised whether or not the United States will need the draft once hostilities in Vietnam have ended. In March 1969 the President appointed a Commission on an All-Volunteer Armed Force "to develop a comprehensive plan for eliminating conscription and moving toward an all-volunteer armed force." The commission reported a year later that it unanimously believed the nation's interest would be better served by an all-volunteer force, *supported by an effective standby draft,* than by a mixed force of volunteers and conscripts. It recommended several steps to move in that direction. The first was "to remove the present inequity in the pay of men serving their first term in the armed forces."

Since that time there has been apparent division between those who, in principle, favor an all-volunteer force and those who, in principle, oppose it. But, examining the debate and the proposals, we find far less difference between those on the two sides in this controversy than many of the headlines and slogans would suggest.

Specifically, the President's commission recommended three things. First, an increase in military pay, particularly for the first two years of enlisted service. Second, comprehensive improvements in the conditions of military service. Third, a standby draft to be activated by joint resolution of Congress upon request of the President.

The President recommended, and Congress enacted, significant pay increases in 1970, and again in 1971. Many of those who favor eliminating draft calls want the draft to continue while the war in Vietnam continues, but they hope and expect draft calls to fall to zero by June 1973, when the present two-year extension will expire. Many who oppose the all-volunteer force express deep misgivings about any system that does not share the risks of combat among all parts of our society; but they have not advocated a policy of low pay in the absence of hostilities or deliberate obstacles to enlistment merely to maintain a draft with armed forces approximately a million men below the peak levels of the late 1960's.

Congressional action on military pay in 1971 does not support the interpretation that those who favor the draft, and those who favor an all-volunteer force, have opposing views on a proper level of military pay, especially for first-term enlistees. The President's commission was

18.

insistent that "the first indispensable step is to remove the present inequity in the pay of men serving their first term in the armed force." No one in the Congress who opposes an all-volunteer force, either an immediate one or an eventual one, has suggested deliberately keeping entry pay low in order to discourage enlistment (although some have indeed opposed reenlistment bonuses of the magnitude of a year's pay or more).

Thus the draft is likely to become a pragmatic question in the next few years. If those who favor an all-volunteer force are correct in their expectations, draft calls may fall to zero, or fall to a level low enough to make a zero draft call attractive. Those who oppose an all-volunteer force, even in the absence of hostilities and at comparatively low troop levels, may face a hard practical question: should voluntary enlistments be deliberately discouraged in order that young men from all walks of life run the risks of two years of peacetime service, and in order that the nonvolunteer components of the armed forces reflect greater diversity in social and economic origins?

Alternatively, if hostilities should continue, both sides in the controversy will largely agree that the all-volunteer force is either not desirable or not achievable (and, in any case, the standby draft that is a basic part of the all-volunteer force proposal of the President's commission would then be in operation).

The Different Issues

We see at least four different issues here that need to be distinguished. The first is whether the draft should in principle be preferred *while hostilities continue*. A second is whether the draft should continue *in the absence of hostilities* when the size of the armed forces has been brought below two and a half million men—below any figure that has obtained since before the Korean War. A third is whether or not to favor substantial *pay increases*, especially for new enlistees, for any of several reasons, but with the probable effect of raising the number of "true volunteers" after hostilities have ended, and with the possibility—doubted by some but expected by others—that with present enlistment standards the armed forces could then be entirely manned by volunteers. And the fourth is whether, if it should prove possible to eliminate draft calls and man the armed services exclusively with volunteers, we should abolish the entire draft system or preserve it on some kind of standby basis.

The President recommended and the Congress concurred that the draft should be continued, at least for a period roughly corresponding to varying estimates of how long the war in Indochina may last.

On the question of pay increases, we strongly agree that there are many reasons for raising military pay, particularly for draftees and new enlistees. And among those reasons are the prospects of reducing reliance on the draft once the war has come to a close, and the size of the armed forces has been substantially further reduced.

On the question whether a continuing draft is necessary or desirable in the ensuing period, *we see no sensible way to determine conclusively whether an all-volunteer force or an indefinitely continuing draft should be the American system for meeting its military manpower needs.* We see no way of forecasting the emergencies that can arise which may either increase the demand for troops or affect the supply of volunteers. We know of no reliable techniques of forecasting, for several years ahead, just what combination of pay, allowances, and conditions of military service will prove attractive to the right numbers and the right kinds of men and women. Either a continuing draft, or a sustained effort to minimize or eliminate the draft, will require annual efforts at carefully integrated terms and conditions of military service, including military pay. But this is not the kind of issue that ought to be resolved once and for all. It is the kind that, in one way or another, must be continually and systematically reexamined in the annual legislative cycle.

Standby Draft

There will always be potentially available a "standby draft." Unless it were put out of reach by Constitutional amendment, which no one has seriously proposed, a draft can be legally instituted almost as quickly as a bill can be drawn up and the Congress convened. If there is no draft law in force, there will be one ready to be activated by Presidential declaration or by quick Congressional response to a President's request. If there is no law on the books, we have no doubt that a draft bill will be ready for quick introduction. The question is essentially one of how much of the present Selective Service System, involving registration and classification, local draft boards, lottery paraphernalia and a host of administrative regulations, will be preserved; or what kind of alternative standby apparatus will be provided.

There appear to be at least three different notions about the status of the draft in the event that draft calls should fall to zero. One, suggested by the term "'zero draft," is that draft calls will be zero but the authority will continue intact, perhaps with a legislated ceiling of zero that can be amended by Congressional action, but with registration continuing, lottery numbers being assigned, registrants being classified, and a continuing definition of the "eligible pool" in terms of age groups.

A second position is that the entire Selective Service System should be dismantled, with the determination not to reinstate any such system except in dire emergency, with draft registration eliminated and a strong commitment to the principle of an all-volunteer force.

A third position, in between, is to preserve a standby draft, with registration and classification but with special procedures required to activate actual conscription. Not only would Presidential declaration or joint Congressional resolution be required to activate the draft, but the procedures for registration and classification would be amended to reflect the expectation that a significant period might pass, perhaps an indefinite period, in which no one would be actually conscripted, and with the expectation that any resumption of draft calls would entail a reexamination of eligibility, selection procedures, deferments, and other terms of service.

In the event that draft calls fall to zero for some period of time, we do not recommend abolishing the Selective Service System altogether. We doubt whether anyone can confidently predict how readily volunteers will be obtained or how satisfactory an all-volunteer force would be. We doubt whether the lives and expectations of young men would be any less disrupted by a system that abolished the draft only to leave uncertain what kind of draft might be hastily reassembled in an emergency or reluctantly reconstructed if the all-volunteer system failed to work satisfactorily. Even if zero draft calls were achieved during a significant period, we are not so confident that they could be indefinitely maintained that we would wish to make resumption of the draft appear an abrupt reversal. We would not even like to see a near-successful all-volunteer period so dramatically reversed and discredited just because it proved necessary for a few years to augment the force with draftees.

We do think that a standby draft might well be different from the present draft. **Specifically, we propose that any draft be subject to a regular decision by the Congress on the number of men to be so inducted.** We doubt whether the present terms of the draft would be maintained in detail. We favor requiring Congressional action in response to a Presidential request in order that the draft be resumed. But sheer orderliness suggests that legislation be kept up-to-date on the books and ready for activation, and that eligible young men know where they stand from year to year or from month to month in the event that draft calls are resumed.

Furthermore, reactivation of the draft, after a period of zero draft, could occur *either* in response to a sudden emergency *or* in the light of cumulative developments that made the draft appear a necessary part of a longer-term manpower policy.

Even in response to sudden emergency, no draft provides trained men instantly in the places where they are needed. The Congress should not merely enact or activate a standby draft but should consider the size of the draft and the kind of draft that makes sense in view of the numbers to be drafted, the likely duration of the need, and the impact of the draft on the economy. Questions of equity and morale will arise, especially if there is a sudden enactment of the draft or sudden enlargement after a period of zero or near-zero draft calls, or if the sudden enlargement is expected to be temporary and relatively few young men are to be caught in it. The question of how to distribute the draft among age groups, for example, is something that the Congress would wish to decide, on a recommendation by the President, rather than to be silent on. The draft is not the first resort when trained manpower is needed in an emergency. The reserves should be in readiness for quick call to active duty. So, typically, there will be time to consider these questions. And the best time to consider them is regularly—in the course of an annual manpower review, when the latest trends can be studied and likely contingencies reviewed.

22.

3.

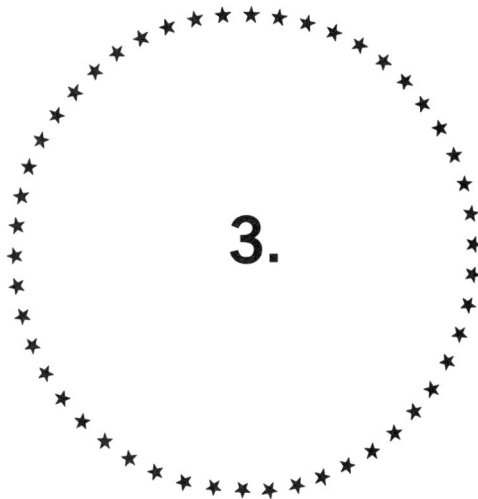

Proposal for an Annual Review
of Military Manpower

        The Congress has been increasingly concerned with its role in the determination of foreign policy, especially where military commitments are involved. The Constitutional responsibility of the Congress to raise armies and to declare war, and the President's powers as Commander-in-Chief, have been subject to ambiguous and conflicting interpretations.

        Congressional authority over the procurement of military manpower—authorizing troop levels, setting pay scales, and legislating the provisions of the draft—is comparatively clear-cut. Lacking, however, has been some systematic and responsible means for the Congress to regularize the authorization of overseas manpower commitments.

        This expressed need of the Congress to find a way to participate in decisions on commitments abroad, especially those represented by

23.

the stationing of American troops, strongly motivated this Committee to consider, and now to propose, a regularized procedure for an annual military manpower review.

A prerequisite for a sound defense policy, one that has the confidence of the American public and of its elected representatives, is some institutional framework that generates informed public debate about the national security benefits and costs of alternative military policies. Such a debate must be focused in the Congress. While public discussion of general principles of strategy and policy might seem desirable, experience strongly suggests that legislation is the best vehicle for serious debate of issues such as authority to deploy troops overseas, to draft young men into military service, and to spend tens of billions of dollars in military pay and allowances.

Direct military personnel costs—pay and allowances—are more than a third of the entire defense budget. With civilian pay, the total personnel costs come to more than half. For two decades, over two and a half million men and women have been in uniform. Indirectly, many other costs in the defense budget relate to the training and maintenance of active-duty personnel. This is an exceedingly complex personnel system, with problems unique to the military, and impinging on a large civilian staff. It involves lifetime careers, short tours of duty, the line of demarcation between civilian and military personnel, and questions of equity, efficiency, and parallelism among military services. **Just as procurement obligations are budgeted annually, so should the civilian-military manpower plan of the Department of Defense be reviewed annually in the context of long-term projections.***

A democratic government should be held accountable after the fact for the money it has spent, as well as having to justify in advance its budgetary proposals. Similarly, it should be held accountable after the fact for the use it has made of the manpower entrusted to it, and should have to justify in advance its plans for recruitment and, especially, conscription.

It should also be recognized that the management of military manpower has major impact on the labor force and on our educational systems. A full and regular accounting can provide a unique source of invaluable demographic data. The fullest disclosure compatible with

---

*See Memorandum by MR. PHILIP SPORN, page 39.

24.

national security should be as regularly forthcoming with respect to manpower as with respect to budget funds. (For the latter there is already a formalized Congressional responsibility represented in the General Accounting Office.) Even problems of race relations and drug abuse can benefit from timely disclosure in an annual proceeding with appropriate committees of the Congress. The privacy of executive session can be employed where necessary.

The Executive Branch presently has no straightforward way of obtaining express Congressional support of military commitments, especially those involving the overseas deployment of troops. Ad hoc resolutions of Congressional endorsement can occasionally be sought, as with the deployment of troops to NATO Europe in the early 1950's, the Gulf of Tonkin Resolution, the Eisenhower Doctrine for the Middle East or the Formosa Doctrine, and (by the Senate alone) on the occasion of treaty ratification. But emergencies aside, Presidential requests for Congressional endorsement of overseas military commitments have the character of gratuitous and extraordinary actions that correspond to no regular governmental procedures—actions that may seem to imply a concession by the President that he lacks authority to deploy or to redeploy troops or to incur Executive agreements. At the same time, Congressional efforts either to sustain Presidential action or to restrain it often have the character of confrontation, as evidenced by the fact that legislative riders to inappropriate or irrelevant legislation are so frequently the vehicle chosen for such efforts. The Congress can challenge dramatically a Presidential deployment of troops, making it an either-or issue; but it cannot so readily express its own intention without appearing to take sides on a major direction of American policy.

The Congress has recently considered enacting procedures to be followed by the President in the event that he substantially enlarges military forces already located in a foreign nation or newly commits U.S. military forces to foreign territory. The principle of requiring a prompt report by the President and a formal request for continuing authority is basically sound and does not encroach on the Constitutional powers of the President as Commander-in-Chief. Such a procedure does, however, require a base line from which to measure new or enlarged troop deployments in foreign countries and by which to judge whether new commitments are incurred.

Annual authorization of overseas troop commitments would

constitute such a base line. These procedures should not limit the President's power to act as Commander-in-Chief in an emergency; they can require of the President an after-the-fact accounting for his action, affording the Congress an opportunity—even imposing on the Congress an obligation—to concur or to impose limitations on the commitments so incurred.

In 1971 the Congress foresaw the coming question of what we as a nation should do about the draft, but did not decisively act upon it. The Congress extended Selective Service for two more years and substantially raised enlistees' pay. The President has recommended measures that he hopes will reduce draft calls to zero by the end of the fiscal year 1972-73. Because of the war in Vietnam and the uncertainties about its course, he and many in the Congress who support an undrafted peacetime army were still unwilling to commit themselves to the elimination of draft calls. Many in the Congress are dubious about the feasibility—and the appropriateness if feasible—of an "all-volunteer" military force even in peacetime. But the issue did not have to be decided in 1971, and it was not decided. It cannot be postponed many more years. Decisions presently taken—on military pay, for example— necessarily reflect expectations about the future role of the draft.

The Congress furthermore in 1971 expressed its concern about the procurement of men and women for the armed services somewhat the way it regularly and constitutionally expresses its concern about the expenditure of money. It heard the President's proposal and authorized, for the year ahead, active duty personnel strengths for the separate components of the armed forces, just as it regularly and naturally receives Presidential proposals, and authorizes amounts of money to spend.

An open-ended draft was acquiesced in by the Congress while war was in progress during the 1960's. But an open-ended authority to induct people into the armed forces will probably not be accorded the President in peacetime, any more than an open-ended authority to obligate funds. In fact, the Congress in 1971 departed from this policy of an open-ended draft and after receiving and considering the President's recommended figures, legislated numerical limits on the numbers authorized to be drafted in fiscal years 1972 and 1973. This procedure, which clearly represents the Constitutional authority and responsibility of the Congress, was a salutary beginning. It can be built on in years to come.

The Proposal

We believe that an annual review by the Congress of military manpower can play a constructive role in decision making for national security. We believe that such a review is feasible, that it can generate informed debate, that it can provide an incentive for Executive Branch review of manpower needs and overseas commitments, and that it can give the Congress a clearer responsibility with respect to U.S. military strategy and the costs in money and people of supporting that strategy.

We recommend an annual review by the President and the Congress of the sources and uses of military personnel, and Congressional authorization of the military manpower program for the fiscal year.

There is now an annual review of major items of military procurement—aircraft, missiles, tanks, naval vessels and other weapons, together with research and development. We propose a parallel procedure with respect to the two and a half million men and women who comprise the "armed forces" that are equipped with those weapons and that directly cost more than all the weapons and the research and development combined.

Presently the nearest equivalent to such an annual review is the periodic legislation on Selective Service, which this year had appended to it the legislation of troop strengths for the four services for the year to come. Selective Service has been concerned with *one* means of obtaining troops, not with the entire process. Furthermore it is not basically concerned with the deployment of troops, except for the occasional proposals—none actually enacted since 1941—to forbid the deployment of conscripts to combat zones or to overseas areas. Selective Service legislation has not been regularly concerned with the troop levels, enlistments, and reenlistments that together generate the "deficit" to be covered by the draft. Selective Service has furthermore carried a tradition of extension for several years at a time, and as the Chairman of the Senate Armed Services Committee pointed out during the 1971 hearings, there had been no comprehensive reexamination of military manpower during the preceding four years. And prior to 1971 the draft legislation typically followed an "emergency" model that was open-ended with respect to the number of men that the President could draft. The Congress might take an interest in the numbers to be drafted but was not obliged to be legislatively involved in those numbers. Only recently, with the prospect for possibly phasing out the draft itself, has there been a heightened appreciation of the relation between pay scales and the draft.

As we noted earlier, exploratory and tentative efforts were made in 1971 to deal with the question of troop authorization and draft ceilings through a regular annual procedure. For the first time there was a legislative requirement on the President to propose troop-strength figures for the four services, and the Congress for the first time was to authorize those troop strengths by explicit legislation. For the first time in four years, the responsible Congressional committees reviewed the entire question of Selective Service, including the question of whether and when Selective Service itself might go on a standby basis. For the first time the Congress considered an alternative to the open-ended authorization of unlimited inductions, and instead authorized manpower inductions in somewhat the way that it annually authorizes new money to spend.

Yet in 1971 the question of troops abroad committed to NATO was handled in an irregular way, on the floor and not in committee; as a challenge to the status quo rather than as a response to an Executive Branch proposal; as an amendment tacked onto a bill not directly concerned with NATO or with overseas deployments, rather than as a central policy issue straightforwardly presented by the President and responsibly considered through orderly procedures. Troops for Indochina were even more hotly debated in even less straightforward fashion. There was in 1971 no systematic and accepted procedure for dealing with these centrally important issues. There was even no accepted interpretation of how these matters were to be decided. Least of all was there an accepted orderly procedure for Presidential recommendation and Congressional authorization and response.

The Use of Military Manpower

We recommend that, at a minimum, the Congress should explicitly authorize by major overseas areas the numbers of troops that may be deployed outside the United States. This requirement will furthermore provide a responsible occasion for public debate, and an orderly procedure for overseas troop deployment. Constructive and informed debate will require informative and candid submissions by the Executive

28.

Branch, supported by a rationale that relates the deployments to specified policies, commitments and contingencies. (Some testimony would undoubtedly have to occur in executive session, with editing for security before release.)

There will still be challenges to the Administration's commitment of troops to Europe, or to Southeast Asia. But a responsible procedure should permit the Congress to question without necessarily challenging, to compromise rather than to confront, to alter deployments in an orderly fashion over time rather than by sudden drastic shifts of policy, and to assert a posture of unity and decisiveness both at home and abroad.

The Source of Military Manpower

In contrast to the review of deployments, **the Congress should annually consider at least a three-year projection of military manpower sources.** It should do this in a context of pay and bonuses, terms and conditions of enlistment and reenlistment, and a specific recommendation by the President on the number of men to be authorized for induction during the year. **It would be the responsibility of the Congress, on the recommendation of the President, to authorize a specific number as the maximum to be inducted through the draft during the coming fiscal year.** That number could, of course, be zero. The Congress would specify the procedures, too, for revising that ceiling in the event circumstances necessitated revision, upward or downward, in the course of the year. And it would be up to the Congress, at the same time, to determine the nature of the continuing draft system—registration, classification, etc.—even if no inductions are authorized for the year to come.

A "Manpower Budget"

There would thus be, each year, an occasion when the Congress examines its entire military "manpower budget," including not merely the money costs but the men and women themselves. This examination would cover both the *sources* of manpower and the projected *uses* of manpower, particularly the locations of deployment and the commitments to be met. But this would also be the occasion to consider all aspects of military manpower, including the relation of the reserves and the National Guard to the active-duty forces and the relation between the uniformed and the civilian personnel in meeting the manpower needs of the military services.[1]

With respect to authorized overseas deployments, there is no intention of reducing the President's responsibility as Commander-in-Chief. The Congress would legislate not a rigid pattern of deployment but rather a base line from which to measure departures. The Congress may not successfully demand of the President that he act slowly, seeking authority, rather than rapidly in an emergency. It may, however, respond to the President's proposals for a nonemergency deployment of troops overseas. And in the event of Presidential action that departs from the approved troop program, the Congress may properly ask the President to report promptly what he has done, why he did it, the reasons why advance authorization was infeasible or unwise, whether the situation will continue and what it may lead to, and what the implications will be for military manpower, defense budgets, other commitments, and the national economy. There can be no reasonable objection that it interferes with the President's role as Commander-in-Chief to require that he seek Congressional approval of expected peacetime overseas deployments and that he promptly and fully inform the Congress of significant actions involving U.S. troops abroad, including departures from the program that was authorized for the year, and to request the new authority that he considers necessary.

---

[1] A careful annual examination of military manpower by the Congress will require strengthened staff capabilities. The importance of additional resources to meet the informational and analytical needs of Congress has been emphasized in *Making Congress More Effective*, A Statement on National Policy by the Research and Policy Committee, Committee for Economic Development (New York: September 1970), pp. 50, 51.

4.

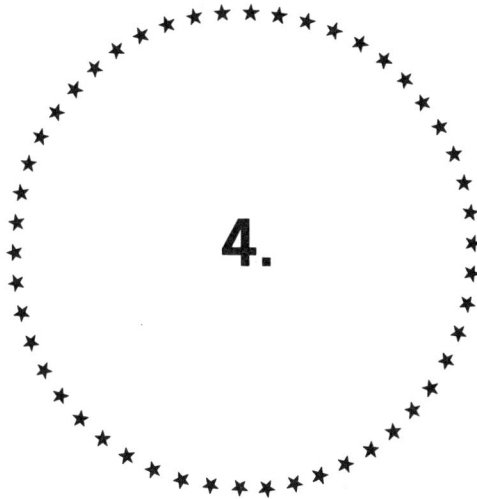

The Proposal in Detail

We propose that Congress require the President to submit annually, early in the calendar year for the coming fiscal year, his recommendations regarding:

1. maximum authorized troop strength, separately for the four military services;[1]
2. maximum authorized overseas deployment of U.S. military personnel, subdivided by region;
3. a specific maximum on the number of men to be drafted during the year;
4. reserve strengths for the fiscal year.*

The President's recommendations should be accompanied by a detailed factual report and justification for the strength levels recom-

---

1/The legislation of *average* active-duty strengths over the fiscal year as presently provided is awkward and leads to ambiguity and uncertainty, especially as to the trend envisaged from the beginning to the end of the year. A numerical ceiling, augmented if desired by an authorized end-of-year strength, would express Congressional intent more straightforwardly.

*See Memorandum by MR. E. B. FITZGERALD, page 40.

mended, in total and overseas, and an explanation of the relationship between the personnel strength levels recommended for the fiscal year and the national security policies of the United States in effect at the time. The President should submit a three-year projection of enlistments, reenlistments and inductions, together with his proposals for military pay and other terms of service, with sufficient supporting detail to justify any numbers to be drafted, any changes in pay and terms of service, and any proposed allocation of draftees among services and regions. In the event that Congressional authorization for a fiscal year is delayed beyond June 30, the limits on active-duty personnel in the several services and stationed overseas proposed by the President should be considered to be in force in the new fiscal year until the new authorizations have been enacted.[2] *

The Military Selective Service Act should be reexamined and appropriately amended every year in the same process that determines the military manpower authorizations and military pay. The number of men authorized to be drafted would be renewed annually. But this is not the only variable that should be reexamined annually in accordance with changing needs and circumstances. Provisions regarding length of service, induction standards, occupational and educational deferments, nonmilitary alternative service, the age profile of the draft-eligible population, specific training requirements, pay and reenlistment bonuses and G.I. benefits, and many other important features of the system will need to be examined annually and modified. Requiring explicit new legislation to extend the system will help to assure that such annual reexamination is considered as a normal part of budget and management, rather than as a challenge to the system itself.

Manpower Procurement

The President should submit detailed manpower procurement projections covering at least three years, including the fiscal year for which authorization is requested. This appears to be the minimum planning period within which any decisions can be taken on the draft, since it includes the period during which men conscripted as authorized

---

2/The problem of lagging authorizations would be reduced if the federal fiscal year were changed to coincide with the calendar year. This change has been recommended by this Committee in the policy statement, *Making Congress More Effective*, pp. 34-40.
*See Memorandum by MR. W. D. EBERLE, page 41.

32.

in the act would be serving their terms. Phased expirations of enlistments, estimated reenlistments, new enlistments and draft calls should be projected at least three years ahead. It will indeed be difficult to estimate in advance the numbers of young men who will offer themselves for enlistment, in view of the multitude of uncertainties surrounding the state of the world and the labor market at home. It is all the more important, therefore, to project with some accuracy the terms of enlistments already in hand, the terms controllable under the draft, trends in reenlistment, and the likely manpower deficiencies by service and by deployment area.

The annual review should concern itself with all the variables that may determine enlistment rates, reenlistment rates, and inductions under the draft. These include a review of the specific skills and experience required among the different services; the physical, educational and moral standards applied by the several services in recruitment; the standards for inducting draftees, specific inducements to reenlistment, the possibilities for "lateral entry" of skilled men and women in specialized categories, and the substitution of civilian employees for uniformed employees. The draft should not be considered the natural or only response to a projected manpower deficit; it is one of several variables subject to control, and not necessarily the most flexible. Specifically, the reserves ought to be, for both military and political reasons, promptly available and ready for active duty.

At the same time, those who believe that the market would always provide an all-volunteer force, if only military wages were allowed to vary with supply and demand, must recognize that there are constraints on military pay scales that just do not apply to the private sector of the economy. The Congress may wish to consider allowing the Executive Branch some flexibility in pay scales, bonuses, induction standards, and other terms of enlistment; but it would be a mistake to compare an all-volunteer force with the labor force in a competitive sector of the private economy.

In the event that Congress authorizes a zero draft for a forthcoming year, it will have to consider how much of the Selective Service apparatus to continue. It can do that only in the light of the prospects for continued nonreliance on the draft. There will usually be no assurance that a draft will not have to be activated in the foreseeable future. The age composition of the draft pool will change according to whether a renewed draft would consider a single year's age group or contain a larger cumulative total. Such questions as whether the draft should be by lottery, and if so whether young men should continue to get their numbers in the face of prospective zero draft calls, and whether such numbers should be in twelve-month slices, can be answered sensibly only when the appropriate time comes. The annual manpower review will regularly provide such a time.

Overseas Deployment

On the overseas deployment side, a different set of considerations apply. First, the need for and feasibility of three-year projections are substantially less. Second, while existing troop levels will rarely be classified for security, plans and contingencies may be loaded with diplomatic significance, if not secrecy, and much of the detail and the justification will have to be discussed in executive session. (There is adequate precedent, in both military and foreign aid authorizations, for requiring the Executive Branch to submit fully detailed supporting justifications, which can if necessary be reviewed in executive session, while confining the legislative authorization to broad aggregates.) Third, there can be no possible pretense that Congressional review of overseas manpower can be done in a wholly dispassionate way: this is where policy differences are sharp and sometimes unreconcilable, and this is where there is least agreement about the line between Presidential and Congressional prerogative.

The purpose of the review, however, is not to make a perfunctory authorization for the record, but to provide a forum for debate and an opportunity for the appropriate committees of Congress to hear and, if necessary, contest the relation of troop deployments to strategic concepts, policies, and international agreements. The debate will depend very much on the Department of Defense's provision of planned deployments and the rationale underlying them.

Only experience will show what degree of detail makes for fruitful examination. It is not easy to predict what leverage the Congressional committees will actually have available in obliging the Executive Branch to be candid, explicit, and informative. But an understanding participation by the Congress in the annual manpower review can in many cases strengthen the diplomatic hand of the President and reduce

34.

misapprehension by other governments of what the United States is committed to do. It can forestall controversy and misunderstanding between the Executive and Legislative Branches of our own government. Furthermore, a responsible regular framework for consideration and commitment by the Congress can help to forestall the more irregular and opportunistic efforts, through legislative riders and other devices, to make a political issue of troop commitments overseas.

Thus, a regular annual procedure can allow the Congress to question overseas deployments without having to challenge their legitimacy and appropriateness.

Emergency Redeployment

As we noted earlier, an established annual review would not inhibit the President from dealing with emergencies. However, the President should be required to seek, whenever feasible, specific authorization from the Congress before taking action inconsistent with the overseas deployment program that the Congress has authorized for the year. In the event that the President substantially departs from that program without prior authorization, he should submit promptly to the Speaker of the House of Representatives and to the President of the Senate a written report setting forth:

1. the circumstances necessitating his action;
2. the Constitutional, legislative, and treaty provisions under the authority of which he took such action, together with his reasons for not seeking specific prior Congressional authorization;
3. the estimated scope of activities; and
4. the President's proposal for legislative revision of the overseas deployment ceilings if the departures in question are expected to last beyond 30 days.

We recommend that Congress then be given 30 days within which to consider the President's new request for legislative authority and to confirm, modify, or deny the President's request by legislative action. Specific procedures should be adopted to assure that any bill or resolution revising the previously enacted troop deployment ceilings could promptly be reported, or considered as reported, from committee and become the pending business of the house to which it is reported, and voted upon within a specified number of days.

If after 30 days the Congress has not acted on the President's request, the President, by so declaring to the Congress, should have the authority to continue to deploy troops overseas within the terms of his new request, until the Congress acts. In the continuing absence of Congressional action, the authority requested by the President would continue in effect to the end of the fiscal year.

Nothing in this procedure is intended to affect the powers the President now has under the Constitution as Commander-in-Chief of the armed forces.

The President's authority, upon declaration of a national emergency, to call units from the ready reserve into active-duty status could continue as at present with a limit on the number of men that can be so called but without regard to the annually authorized active-duty strengths of the four services. The present obligation of the President to report to the Congress when he calls reserve units to active duty, and periodically as long as they remain on active duty, should be continued but might properly be revised somewhat in conformity with the procedure outlined above for emergency departure from the authorized overseas deployments.

Congressional Committee Responsibilities

The Armed Services Committees in both houses should have primary responsibility, as they presently do, for the total service strengths, for reserve strength, and for the draft; and these committees should initiate the necessary legislation. But providing strength for the armed services is only one side of this proposal. The other side is overseas deployment, which is perhaps the most important way for Congress to clarify regularly the status of U.S. commitments abroad and to examine those commitments as embodied in the armed forces of the United States. Therefore the Foreign Relations and Foreign Affairs Committees should both participate in reviewing the President's recommendation for overseas deployment, and in making their recommendations on such authorization to the two houses of the Congress.

This could be done by joint hearings of the two Committees in each house, by sequential consideration of the part of the annual bill that is the business of both Committees, or even by the formation of a joint committee, with members from the Committees on Armed Services and Foreign Relations, to consider the bill as a whole. In the absence of new arrangements for joint consideration of the foreign policy aspects of military manpower between interested committees in each house, we recommend that, in addition to consideration of the entire subject by the Armed Services Committees of both houses, the House Foreign Affairs Committee and the Senate Foreign Relations Committee be responsible for a separate consideration of the foreign policy implications of the President's recommendations, and separately report to their respective houses within a time limit that assures timely action by the House and the Senate.

It is clear that the procedure proposed here will require an unusual degree of coordination and collaboration between the Armed Services and Foreign Affairs Committees in the House. Thus, if this annual manpower review, with its annual examination of overseas deployment, can serve to bring those committees into closer relationship, an extra benefit will have been achieved.

There have been recommendations from several sources for a new joint committee on national security affairs, drawn from both houses of the Congress.[3] We emphasize, however, that the military manpower review should be a central part of the legislative process—culminating each year in authorizing legislation without which funds may not be appropriated for military personnel costs, or men drafted—and must be primarily in the hands of committees responsible for legislation in the field of defense and foreign affairs. We should not like this proposal for an annual military manpower authorizing procedure to founder with any organizational proposals for changing the committee structures of the two houses of Congress. We should welcome, however, any restructuring that would alleviate the present anomaly that defense and foreign affairs, so intimately related in Executive Branch planning and so intertwined in practice, are not comparably coordinated within the committee structures of the Congress.

3/This Committee has addressed the question of Congressional committee organization in the policy statement, *Making Congress More Effective*, pp. 41-51.

Memoranda
★ of Comment, Reservation, ★
or Dissent

Page 9—By JOSEPH COORS:

I am voting against publication of the statement which has been prepared on Military Manpower and National Security because of general disagreement with the fundamental concepts which are represented therein. I believe that the proposals are impractical and unwieldy. They mix up the functions of the Executive Branch and the law-making arm of our government and recommend giving Congress responsibilities far beyond those which are delegated to it by the Constitution. Our government becomes so complex these days that it cannot stand further complications which would arise out of putting Congress further into the administrative function. Our Constitution spells out quite clearly that the Congress is to make the laws and the Executive Branch is to administer them.

More specifically, my objections center around the firm conviction that this proposal would unnecessarily and undesirably interfere with the Commander-in-Chief of our armed services. It would tie his hands and put a stone around his neck in such a way that he could not possibly act adequately to defend our country.

An annual review of numbers in the armed services is generally a waste of time and unworkable. In this rapidly changing world these factors have to be under continual review, not just once a year, by our military leaders. Delay in deployment "to provide a forum for debate and review" would destroy the effectiveness of our military. I view it somewhat like a coach of one team giving his opponent his game plan and signals. It would result in catastrophe. A 30-day limit on a decision by Congress is ridiculous—many wars are won or lost in less time. The whole concept presented in this statement appears to be just another move towards the one-world philosophy which I abhor and which would destroy the United States of America.

38.

Page 9—By RICHARD C. GERSTENBERG, with which MARVIN BOWER, ROBERT B. SEMPLE, and SIDNEY J. WEINBERG, JR. have asked to be associated:

The area being discussed in this CED policy statement is clearly one of great importance to all citizens and is one which deserves the most careful review and analysis. I question, however, whether a CED paper provides the proper forum for such a review and analysis.

In my opinion CED's great contributions have been in the areas of economic policy and particularly with respect to monetary and fiscal policy. Since I do not feel personally qualified to pass judgment on some of the technical analysis contained in this paper, I cannot either support or disagree with a number of these specific policy recommendations.

Page 14—By DONALD S. PERKINS:

The statement does seem to me to overlook the likely future concern of our allies as to their ability to count on us or our President for year to year consistency of support. However, in the face of a strong need for increasing the participative democracy and improving checks and balances in military manpower decision making, I feel that the benefits of the recommendations clearly outweigh the threat of inconsistency.

Page 24—By PHILIP SPORN:

I am in favor of a law requiring Congress to regularize the authorization of overseas manpower commitments. But I am disappointed at the nonchalance with which the question of spending from $35 to $40 billion in defense pay and allowances is treated in the report without any consideration of the serious effect on the country of the additional economic burden on its society as a result of complete elimination of the draft. I know this is being discussed on the basis of no pay differential between draftees and voluntary enlisted, but what social or moral law forces us into adopting so dangerous a policy?

With the end of our manpower commitment to Indochina clearly visible, with a $35 to $40 billion deficit for fiscal 1972 staring us in the face, with the almost certain disappearance of the end-of-the-Vietnam-war dividend we have been looking forward to as a sure reality (instead of the evanescent mirage it will turn out) isn't it time we began to think where we can contract expenditures to make possible implementing the many programs we are doing badly or not at all in such areas as slum elimination, public health, education, environmental pollution, and poverty elimination? Placing our manpower—enrollment, deployment, and costs—under the control of the Congress and doing so on a minimal dollar cost draft basis surely makes much more sense than to go to the other extreme and switch it to a complete volunteer basis. On this the report is silent.

I realize that the recent White House Conference on Youth voted last April to "recommend that the draft law be allowed to expire June 30, 1971" but then it also asked one-quarter of the national budget be allocated to education against the current 3.67%, an increase of some $50 billion per year, and a $6,500 minimum income per year, without any requirement to work, be guaranteed by the government for a family of four, calling surely for at least another $40 billion per year. And it asked for quite a few other programs. But it did not say where the increased funds are to come from at our present rate of productivity. If the Conference on Youth cannot be expected to worry about the economic aspects of such beautiful ideas, surely CED can be, and one of the good places to start is in a discussion of the manpower of our defense forces, a piddling $35 to $40 billion per year item. Or are we expecting too much of CED?

Page 31—By E. B. FITZGERALD:

The real essence of this statement is included in the four proposals detailed on page 31. Proposals three and four recommend a role for Congress in the determination of the size of the draft and reserve strengths. My only comment on these proposals is that the text of the policy statement deals solely with the subject of the draft and I don't believe that it is possible to thus fully consider the matter of the draft without fuller consideration of the roles of the reserves and of the National Guard than is given to these latter organizations in this statement.

The expressed intentions of proposals one and two are to determine the manpower portion of the defense budget in a manner which will reduce misunderstanding between the President and the Congress, which will improve confidence abroad that the President speaks for a unified nation and that will reduce the opportunistic use by Congress of the defense subject for political advantage.

I heartily endorse these intentions and add to them that the manner in which we determine our defense budget should provide additional discouragement to a potential adversary who might be mistakenly tempted to test our defense capabilities.

Unfortunately, the methods proposed to accomplish these intentions will, in my opinion, be counter-productive to their achievement and for this reason I must dissent from proposals one and two.

In actual practice, information on force levels is currently detailed in the Department of Defense budget as submitted to the Congress and is further amplified through testimony by the Secretary of Defense, by the Chairman of the Joint Chiefs of Staff, and by representatives of the individual Services before the cognizant committees of the Congress. In approving the DOD budget, Congress is well-aware of the distribution of forces that the budget is intended to support.

The proposals of this policy statement would deed to the Congress an operational executive function that is contrary to the traditional separation of executive and legislative functions in our government and whose execution would require resources and capabilities within the Congress which do not currently and should not logically exist. Greater rather than less friction between the Congress and the President would appear to be the likely result of this policy of co-determination.

The proposed new role for Congress will likely lengthen the period of defense budget determination, which is already long in relationship to the shifting world conditions to which it must be responsive. Also, the lack of timeliness in Congressional action on detailed defense matters would seriously impede the efficiency of defense operations even under the interim operating authorizations proposed in this statement.

Page 32—By W. D. EBERLE:

I would add that the President must submit his approval no later than March 1 of each year and Congress shall approve this by June 30 of each year. In the event Congress does not approve, the President's recommendations shall be automatically approved for the forthcoming year. This will prevent any attempt to shift responsibility and fix a time certain as this subject is not one that can be delayed.

HONORARY TRUSTEES

TRUSTEES ON LEAVE FOR GOVERNMENT SERVICE

CED PROFESSIONAL AND ADMINISTRATIVE STAFF